I0815006

WORKac

PARK BOOKS

Amale Andraos and Dan Wood, with Miles Hardingwood

Buildings for People and Plants

We don't think of buildings as isolated objects. Rather, we enlist their power to frame, reexamine and reinvent relationships—between citizens and cities, public and private space, the individual and the collective, inside and outside, and people and plants.

When we design buildings, we are constantly asking ourselves questions. Is there a communal or civic potential? What is the project giving back to the city? Who is it for, and can we make it more inclusive? Does it do something for the environment? How can we add meaning or texture or depth? We push every project to do something extra, to make "one plus one equal three." When we design, we are looking for the bonus—always searching for the ways our buildings can be greater than the sum of their parts.

Each building has its own bonus. A library offers after-hours access through a musical ramp. Simple concrete structures use color and space to create a world of possibilities for events, activities, political action, exercise, and job training. A student mailroom becomes an opportunity to reinvent the post office for the twenty-first century and integrate town and gown in new ways. A parking garage becomes an investigation of vertical public space. An office building is carved to create outdoor gardens at every level and public spaces at the ground. A beachfront development becomes a mixed-income study in density and urbanism. A house intertwines art and furniture to foster creative life. An old munitions factory is reimagined as a community resource, keeping the patina of history and combining it with a contemporary interior. A green roof bends and folds to integrate a public building into its neighborhood. Passivhaus standards are used to create a home that is open to nature at every scale.

It is vital to us that we include bonuses whenever and wherever we can. We believe in architecture as a catalyst of progress—and stagnated, unsurprising buildings are the enemy of that progress. It is easy to create the expected, but when you challenge each building to do more, you give it the opportunity to solve problems and provide services—ones that may initially seem incongruous with the project, but that prove to be the perfect fit. No one would have expected a façade to become a playground or a ramp to celebrate community, but these bonuses make the projects what they are—reframing preconceptions to improve the lives of both the building and the people who inhabit it.

Architecture has the power to integrate; to bring things together that are not usually combined. These integrations can result in an element of surprise, a moment of delight, a spark of inspiration. We try to make buildings that jolt people out of their day-to-day lives with an invitation to discover new relationships and possibilities. Sometimes that looks like an unexpected form, material, or color. Sometimes it is about the inclusion of art. Often it is plants. These "jolts" keep our buildings fresh and their inhabitants engaged long after they move in.

For us, color is a material. Some people argue that architecture should express a "pure form" and remain colorless and autonomous from its everyday use. We like to acknowledge that life is, in fact, in color. Color can ground a project. It is about the messiness of life, celebrating the everyday, and not being precious. For us, plants are a material, too. In the same way that color blurs the boundaries around what is considered architecture, plants are organic and alive—and therefore provide a similar jolt of energy and difference when used in a building.

We try to maintain a childlike sense of wonder, both in our design process and our finished projects. That feeling that you are witnessing something different or special, for the first time, makes you feel alive, like you can continue to grow. We believe that play is progressive, so our commitment to continuous evolution and play is a way of insisting that change is possible.

The Gift

Our goal is always to lead with generosity. We want our buildings not to be isolated monoliths, but gifts to the worlds they inhabit. There are many ways a building can be a gift, by embracing sustainability, creating new public spaces, preserving historic structures, or registering the particulars of a site, and paying homage to locality. We also insist on the possibility of shared values across cultures and contexts and believe design can give back by helping people overcome their fear and mistrust of the new, the different, and the unexpected.

We believe it is crucial to try to create a more sustainable world, and that world can be achieved in a myriad of ways. Density and preservation are just as important to sustainability as technological advancements. So is urbanism. If every building contributes in some perhaps unique way, then a neighborhood or city can slowly pivot, and the collective can pave the way for a sustainable future.

Listening is a skill, and community is the backbone of architecture. We work to integrate our projects into the neighborhoods they inhabit. We listen to the voices of the people who will use them. We are flexible to a fault and understand that the most important job of a building is to serve the people who inhabit it.

We have to believe that the world can change because, as architects, we are always making things that don't yet exist. Evolution is possible: for the environment, for equality, for communities. Architecture can be an agent for this transformation, which means architects have a duty to be shepherds of it. And leading with generosity is how we achieve that, through incremental gifts that combine to create real change.

A gift is beautiful in so many ways. The acts of giving and receiving are transformative, as is the beauty of what is being exchanged. In our office, we talk about beauty all the time. Everyone deserves to be surrounded with beauty. Beauty can enhance life, but it is also about care. When you feel like you are part of something that has received thought and attention, the architect's care is palpable.

Nicolai Ouroussoff

Civics Lessons for an Uncertain Future

It's been tough times for New York architects with a civic conscience. Many of the most ambitious (and lucrative) architectural undertakings of recent memory have been sponsored by quasi-authoritarian or autocratic regimes overseas. Meanwhile, in the democratic West, decades of government austerity have made the kind of ambitious public works projects that were once a staple of architecture a distant memory.

So the ten projects in this book, completed between 2017 and 2024, may come as a surprise to some. Visually, their snappy pop-inspired structures, often assembled out of everyday industrial materials and painted in loud florid colors, take their cues from the 1960s and 1970s, a time in the West when the social contract was disintegrating, and architecture was abandoning whatever was left of its social idealism. And yet under the colorful packaging, these projects are informed by a stubborn determination to reengage what is left of the public sphere. Their uplifting message is that architecture, when done right, can not only elevate our everyday experiences; it can also have a meaningful social impact at a time when the civic bonds that hold us together can often seem frayed beyond repair.

Andraos and Wood first met in 1998, when Andraos was a student at Harvard's Graduate School of Design, in Rem Koolhaas's pioneering "Project in the City" studio, and Wood was working for Koolhaas. The following year, Andraos joined Wood in the Rotterdam office, then a magnet for young talent. The couple stayed four years, stockpiling ideas, before moving to New York City, where they eventually opened their own office in the one-bedroom apartment where they lived in Greenwich Village.

It was a volatile time, both in the world and in architecture. As the city was struggling to recover from the shock and trauma of the September 11 terrorist attacks, it was pressing ahead with plans to rebuild at Ground Zero. Meanwhile the pace of globalization was accelerating, and architects were turning their attention to Asia, where the Chinese government had commissioned an impressive array of architectural landmarks in preparation for the Beijing Olympics.

Like other young architects of their generation, Andraos and Wood started out chasing cultural commissions and the kind of high-end luxury projects that can help to pay the bills. The first glimmerings of their approach appear in a winning design for a temporary pavilion for the MoMA/PS1 Young Architects program. Erected in PS1's outdoor courtyard for six months in the summer and fall of 2008, the pavilion was conceived as an urban oasis, bringing together local chefs, farmers, artists, architects, and other assorted creative types. More than two-hundred barrel-shaped cardboard planters were lifted on muscular columns to form an informal shelter for outdoor parties and events. A cistern connected to the museum's roof drainage collected rainwater that was used to irrigate the planters, which were stocked with peas, bean poles, lettuce, tomatoes, and other vegetables; the vegetables were served in the museum's café.

The pavilion eventually drew the attention of John Lyons, the head of Miramax at the time, who was working with the California-based activist-chef Alice Waters, to bring Waters's "edible education" program to New York. They were commissioned to design the first East Coast Edible Schoolyard at P.S. 216 in Brooklyn. Conceived as a kind of pedagogical device, the project includes a greenhouse where the students grow vegetables and fruit and an adjoining classroom-kitchen building where they learn about sustainable food culture. Auxiliary services like mechanical systems, bathrooms, a cistern, and a tool shed are sorted into a series of irregular volumes and plugged into the back. These structures are enveloped in various pop culture references. The blue of the service volumes, for example, is the same tint of sky blue used by Rogers and Piano on the rear façade of the 1977 Centre Pompidou in Paris. The abstract floral pattern of overlapping cement shingles used to decorate the kitchen shed is a direct reference to Venturi and Scott Brown's Best Products Showroom, a postmodern icon completed a year later in Bucks County, Pennsylvania.

But while Rogers and Piano were tapping the rebellious energy of 1960s and 1970s youth culture, and Venturi and Scott Brown were nodding to a suburban American landscape of shopping malls and parking lots, WORKac's design celebrates the multiethnic utopia of urban Brooklyn.

Andraos and Wood would elaborate on this visual language six years later in a design for a parking structure in Miami's Arts District. This time, the architects placed all the structure's vertical circulation in a narrow slot directly behind the façade's perforated metal screen. Painted hot pink, the slot was then packed with a variety of other functions—a climbing gym, lending library, bar, garden, and inflatable pool. Big amoeba-shaped openings are carved out of the perforated screen, allowing partial views through the slot into the garage. Seen from the street, the structure resembles a living billboard—or a gigantic Barbie Dream House still wrapped in its packaging.

If projects like the Miami parking garage point to a mischievous streak in their work, a trio of public libraries, completed in a brief period between 2017 and 2024, testify to their determination to remain socially engaged. The first of these, the renovation and expansion of an existing cut-rate "dumb Modernist box" in Kew Gardens Hills, Queens, was commissioned as part of Mayor Michael Bloomberg's Design Excellence program, which sought to match rising architectural talents with the design of civic works in underserviced neighborhoods. Touted as a new urban model, the program was crippled by bare-bones budgets, bureaucratic red tape, and convoluted landmarks and zoning regulations. Forced to keep costs to a minimum, Andraos and Wood pushed for a zoning variance, allowing them to envelop the existing building and a surrounding lawn in a second skin of corrugated prefabricated concrete panels. The space between new and old was used to house new reading rooms and staff offices; a "green" roof tilts down to one corner, where it connects to a small public garden. The corrugated façade, which resembles a pleated concrete curtain, is lifted on big V-shaped concrete braces at two corners, as if beckoning the Orthodox Jewish community on one side and the Southeast Asian community on another.

Their design for the Adams Street Library is a similar exercise in community building. Like Kew Gardens Hills, it sits at the convergence point of distinct urban neighborhoods, with gentrified Dumbo to the west, the Italian American neighborhood of Vinegar Hill to the east, and Farragut public housing project a few blocks to the south. Here, however, the architects had to slip the library into the first floor of a landmarked former munitions factory, below seven floors of luxury coop apartments. Unable to make binding alterations to the exterior, the architects painted the word LIBRARY in bold white letters onto a fire engine brick façade in a deadpan style reminiscent of an Ed Ruscha word painting. Tucked into the first floor below seven floors of condos, the library itself was organized by age, with adults and teens flanking the perimeter and a children's area at its core. The latter is partly hidden behind a curtain-like wall and raised on a platform, with views to the East River.

Over time, as the architects became more established and the budgets got bigger, the geometries got more complex. Yet the interest in how public buildings can serve as places of common ground remains. The site of their North Boulder Public Library, in Colorado, is an awkward trapezoidal lot bordered by a (mostly white) cookie-cutter development of low-rise apartment blocks and townhouses to the north and a mostly Spanish-speaking community of prefab homes and trailer parks to the east. Andraos and Wood laid out the main floor in an elongated diamond-shaped pattern, with big barn-like reading rooms overlooking a small park and children's playground to the south. The library's roof plane is cut diagonally in two, with one half clad in aluminum panels and supporting solar panels and the other ramping down from a second-floor community center to a point at the site's western-most edge, knitting the building into Broadway to the west, a commercial strip of mini-malls, shops, and liquor stores.

In 2017, Andraos and Wood were hired to design their first major residential development, a seafront community called Marea in Andraos's native Lebanon. The country's economy was then on an upswing, and Beirut was awash in high-profile architectural projects, part of an effort to revitalize the city center. Located a one-hour drive to the north, near the site of a former Syrian military checkpoint and next door to the ancient coastal city of Batroun, Marea was conceived as an oasis of calm, one that seemed to confirm that the country had moved on from its war-torn past. Clad in uniform white terrazzo panels that glimmer in the Mediterranean light, the units stagger down a hillside, with studio apartments at the top and larger villas along the beach below. A network of alleyways, shared courtyards, and private patios cut through these forms at odd angles, so that from a distance it looks as if the entire development were carved from a single faceted block.

The reassuring message seems to be that the individual cannot be separated from the collective whole. And yet the severe abstraction of the forms, stripped of unnecessary detail, tells us that all communities are intellectual constructs, and thus as fragile as the values that bind them together.

Of course, we now know how fragile those ties can be. As I write, bombs are falling on Beirut and families are fleeing to the north. Everywhere you look, the bonds that once held people together are on the verge of being permanently severed. In these times, WORKac's work is a reminder that it is possible to foster new forms of association, if only we can find the will.

Left: Edible Schoolyard NYC at P.S. 216, Brooklyn, 2014
Right: Public Farm 1, PS1 MoMA, Queens, 2008

North Boulder Library

2024

Boulder, Colorado

NoBo

EXIT

Sedaris
SMITHSONIAN
ASIAN PACIFIC
AMERICAN
OBJECTS
EMPRESS
LYNNE OLSON
WALDEN
NIGHTBIRDS
PROMISE BOYS
ARTIFICE

Aprendo números
Richard Scarry's
100
FIRST WORDS

PICTURE BOOKS

STAFF PICKS

Welcome!
ARTIST
MEET AND

Pilares Lomas de Becerra
and Azcapotzalco

2023
Mexico City, Mexico

RUTA DE EVACUACION

RUTA DE EVACUACION

ACTIVIDADES CULTURALES GRATUITAS
PILARES
LOMAS DE BECERRA
TEATRO
Stop-E
SON JAROCHO
Artes Plasticas
Y muchas mas...
Bienvenidos
Actividades Gratuitas

INSTITUTO
PONTE PILA

PILARES
PARA EL BIENESTAR

ÓN, LIBERTAD, ARTE, ED ACIÓN Y SA
39
39

RISD Student Success Center

2019
Providence, Rhode Island

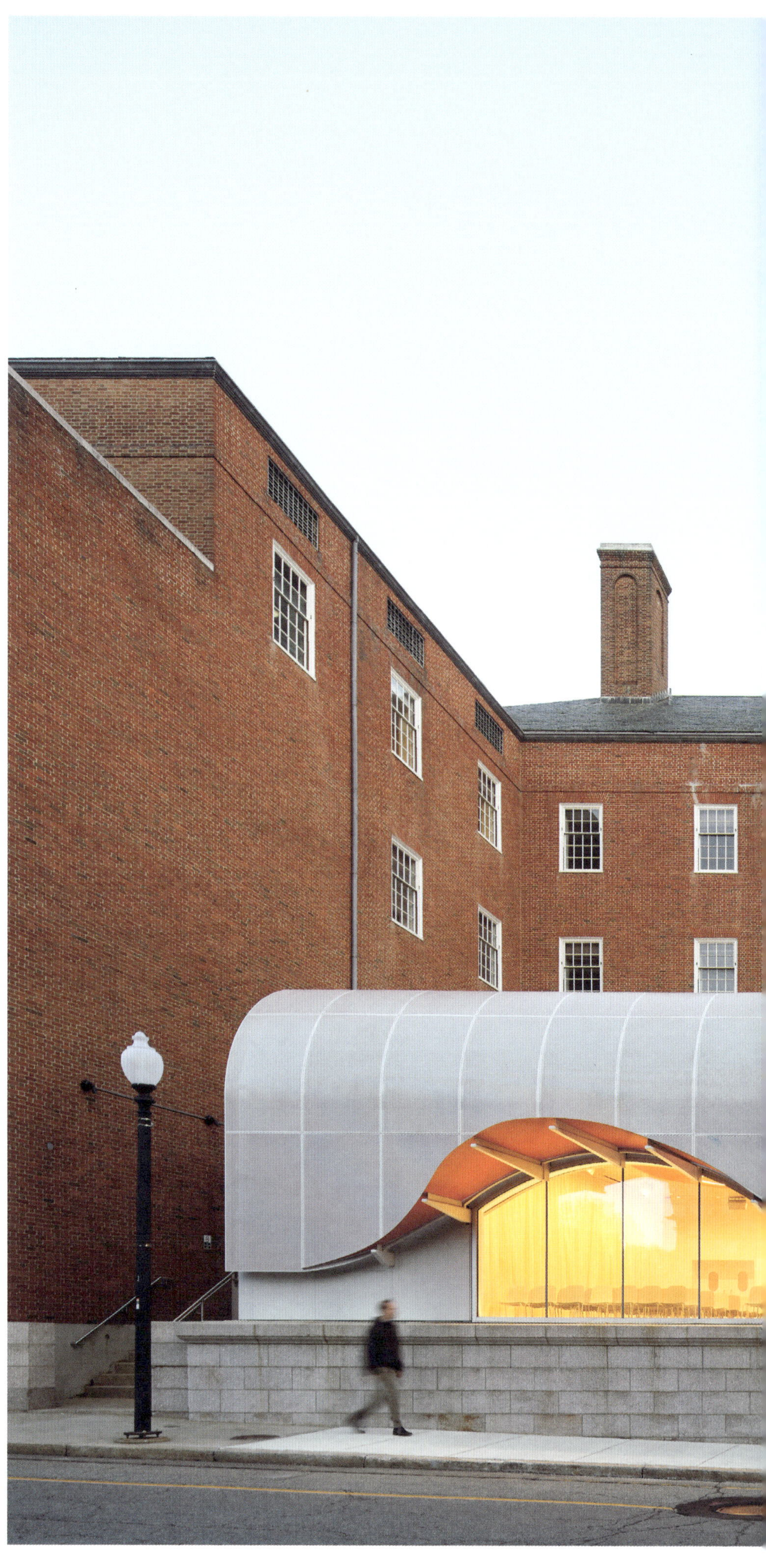

ANY TIME
NO PARKING

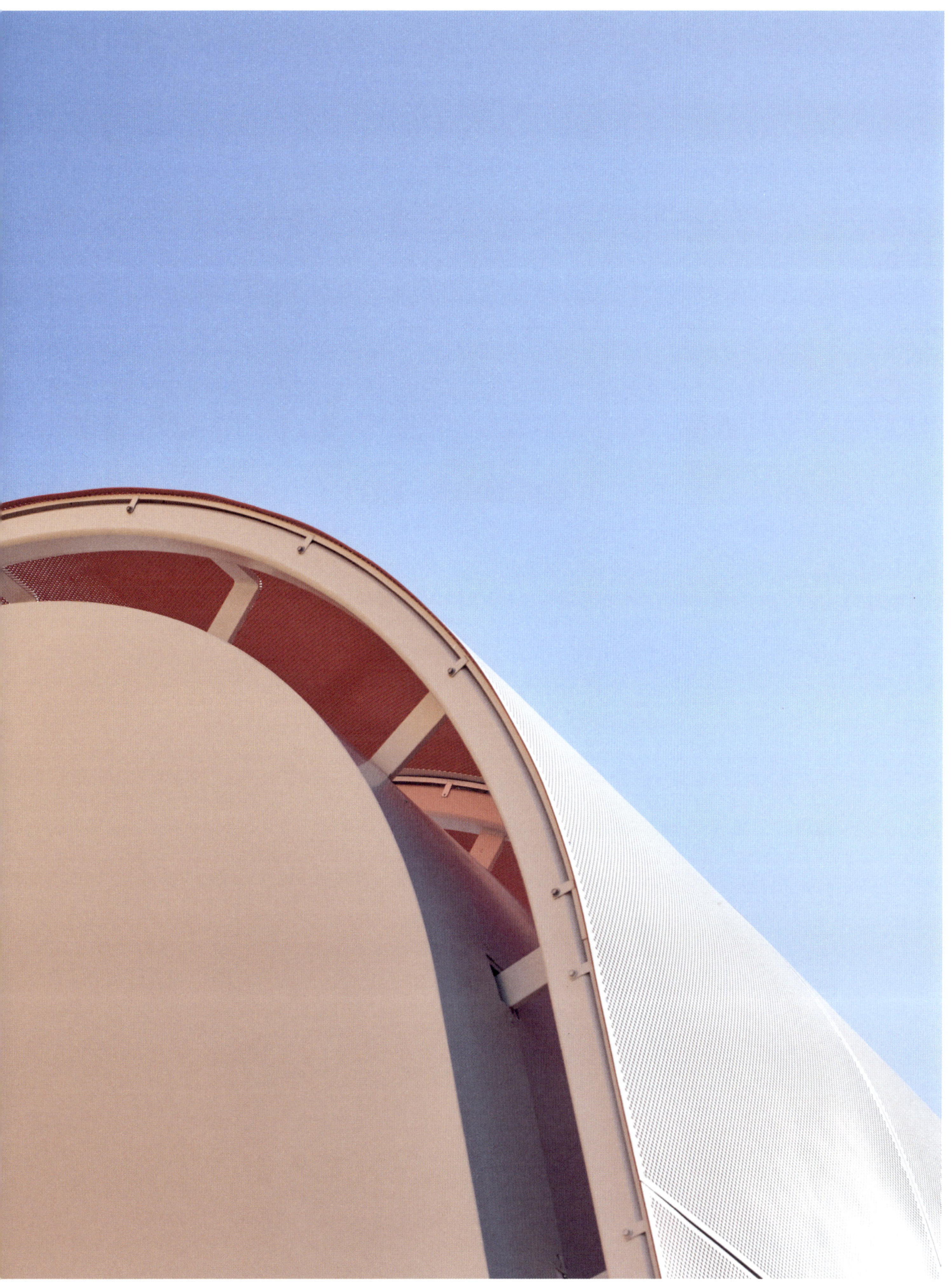

CAREER
CENTER

THANK YOU!

RISD
20 WASHINGTON PLACE
CAUTION
STAND CLEAR

Miami Museum Garage

2018
Miami, Florida

CAR ACCIDENT?

Sable

Mission Rock Building B

2024

San Francisco, California

Channel
280
South
+1 415 772 0306
[LUXFIT]

[LUXFIT]
[LUXFIT]
[LUXFIT]
[LUXFIT]
[LUXFIT]
[LUXFIT]

Marea

2021
Batroun, Lebanon

Villa Papillon

2022
Batroun, Lebanon

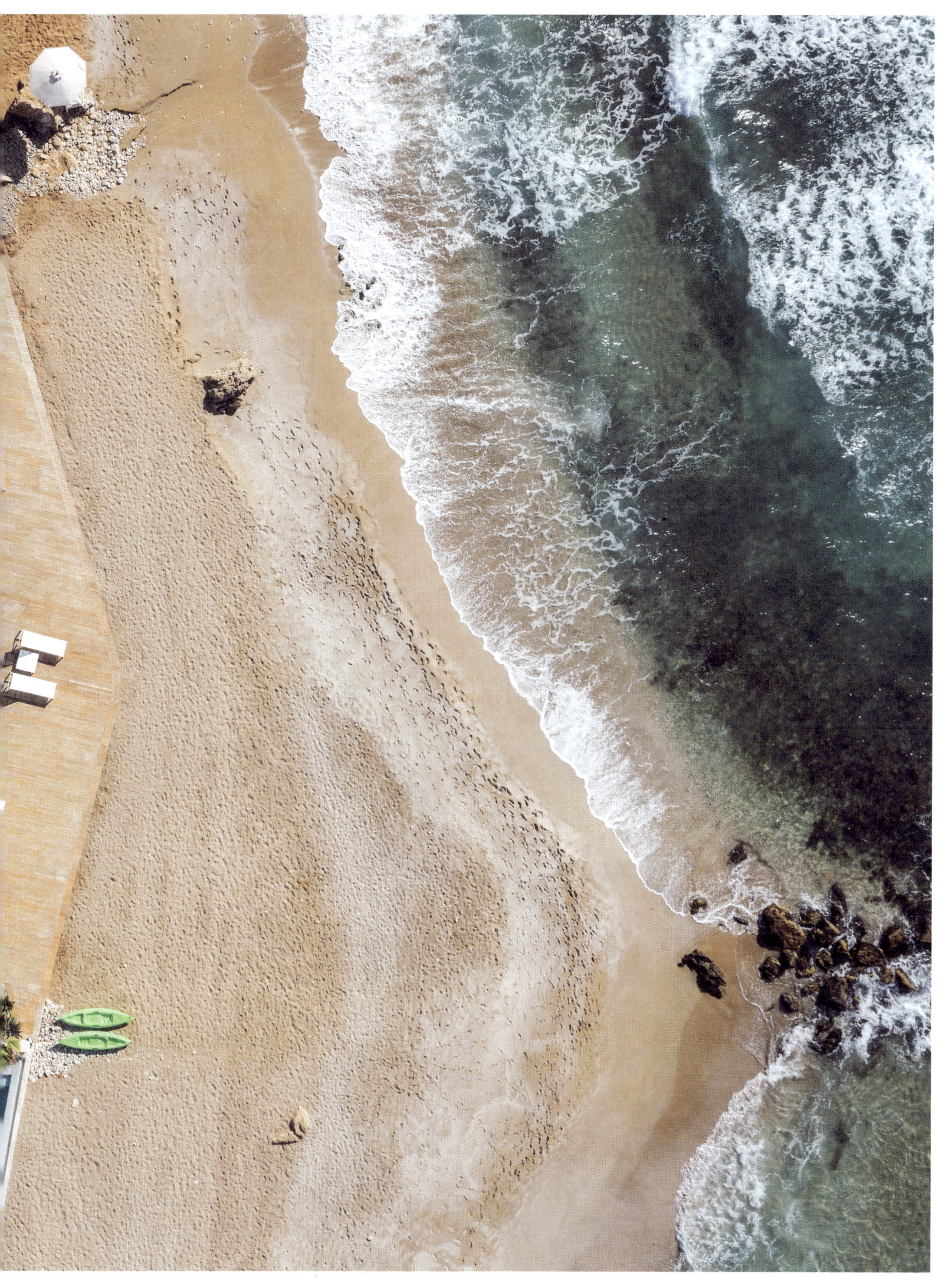

OH
SHIT

Adams Street Library

2021
Brooklyn, New York

LIBR

ARY
Adams St
ONE WAY

LIBRO COSTURA

World Language
World Language
World Language

Picture Books
Picture Books

llama
llama
red
pajama

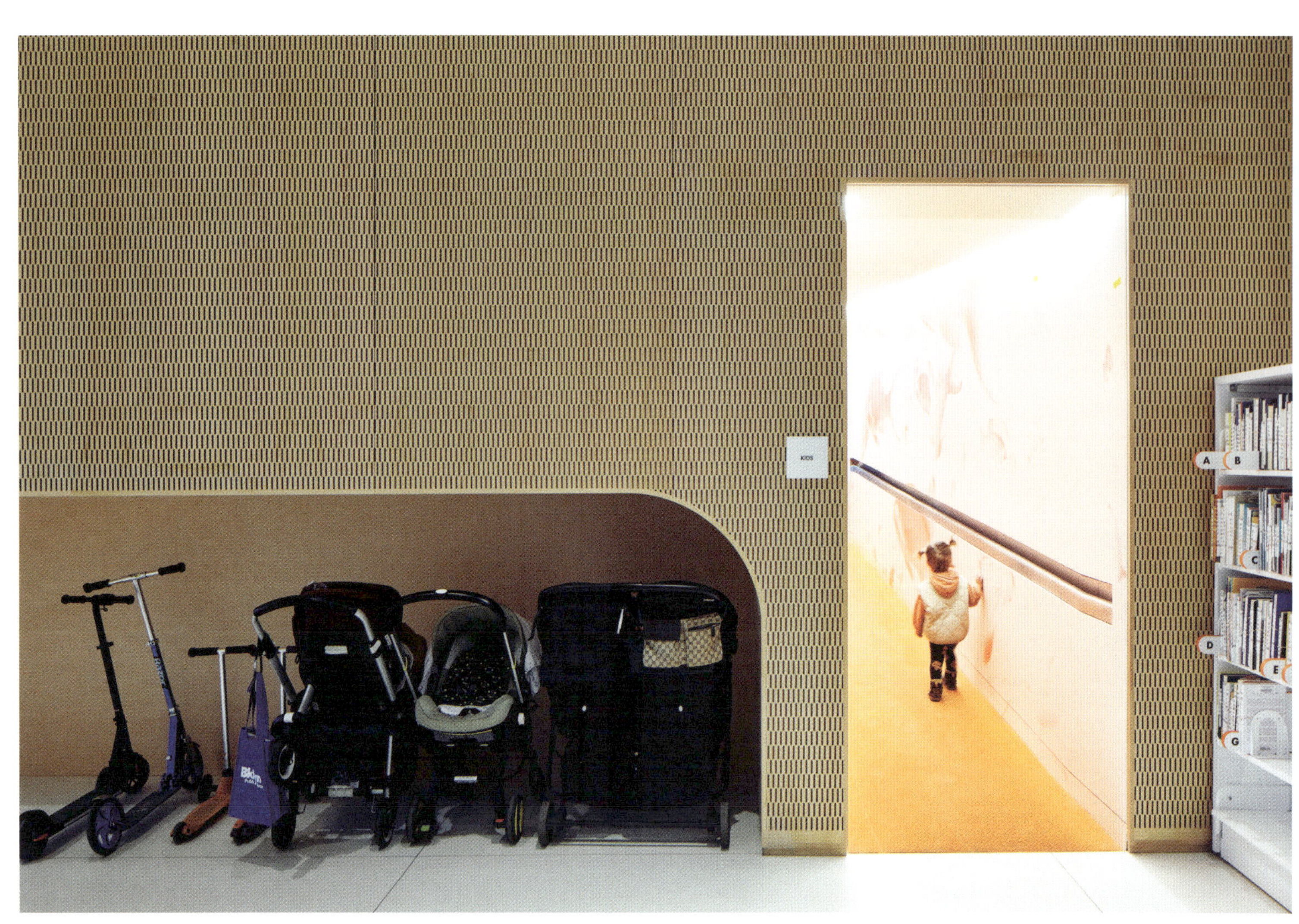
KIDS

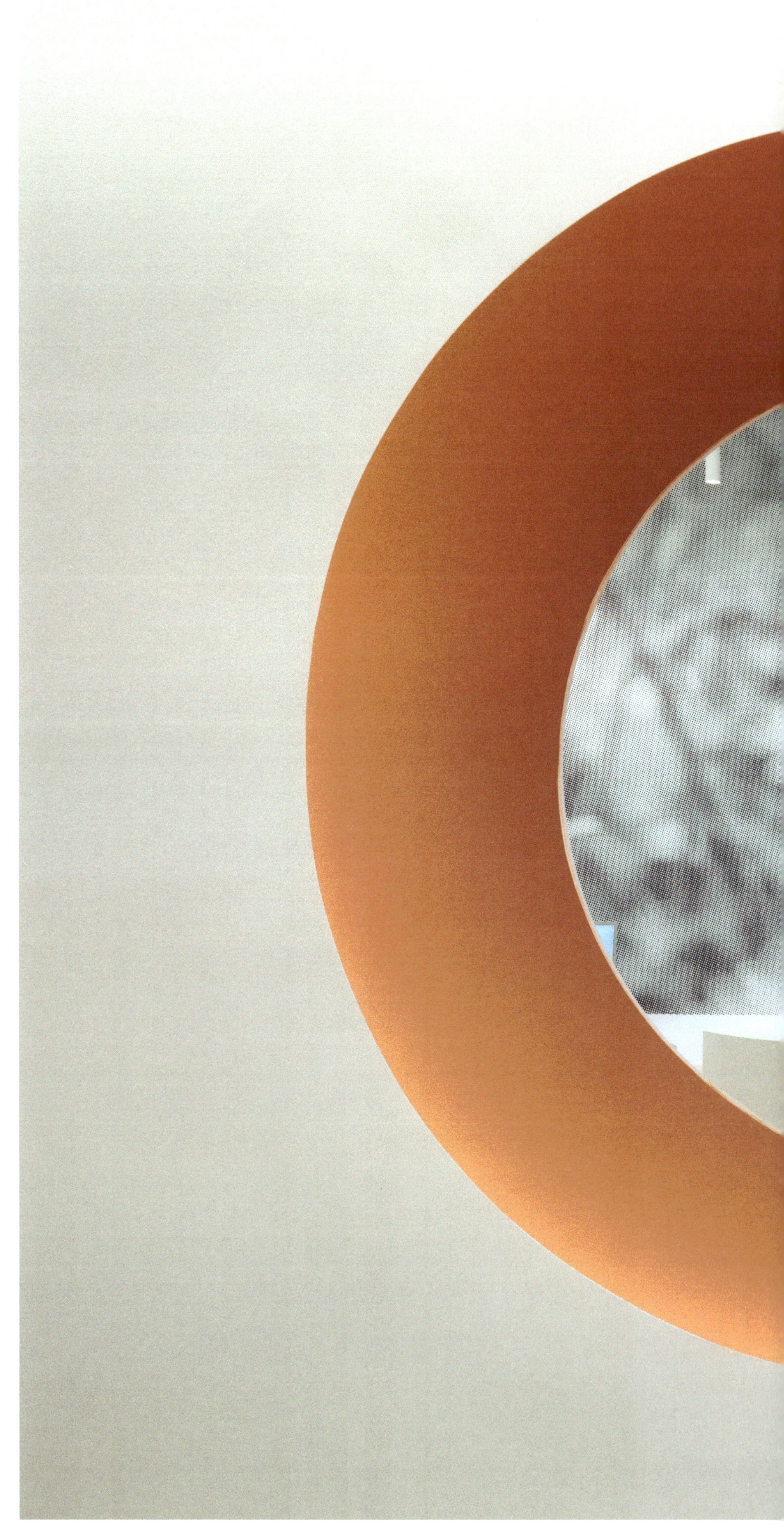

RETURNS

Kew Gardens Hills Library

2017
Queens, New York

LIBRA

ONE WAY
ONE WAY

DENTIST

LIBRARY
SMILES
QUEENS LIBRA

QUEENS LIBRARY
KEW GARDENS HILLS

EXIT
TEENS

Jewish Reference
IS IT KOSHER?

LEIGH PL
at Dolan
WAY

Riverhouse

2025
Hopkinton, Rhode Island

Drawings and Stories

The North Boulder Library, nestled at the base of the Rocky Mountain foothills with a clear view of the Boulder Flatirons, is the product of extensive community outreach and perseverance through the pandemic. The diverse and unique neighborhood of North Boulder—which contains a Spanish-speaking population, two manufactured home communities, families with young children, new condos, and artists' studios and galleries—inspired the building's form, program, and orientation. Large windows open to the south, with spectacular views from the main reading rooms. The building's more restrained north façade respects the scale of its residential neighbors. Here, a lower roof doubles as an accessible entrance to the second floor, connecting Broadway directly to classrooms and community rooms, allowing them to remain open after hours. The ramp incorporates a musical installation by Daily Tous Les Jours that creates melodies as sensors register people walking up or kids dancing. This embrace of play extends to the children's area, where a climbing net and a slide are integrated into the façade. Solar panels, increased insulation, and hyper-efficient mechanical systems ensure the building exceeds Boulder's elevated sustainability standards.

Year	2024
Location	Boulder, Colorado
Size	13,000 SF
Project Team	Nevin Blum Matt Voss Troy Lacombe with Leslie Dougrou Anne Erichsen Kelly Lee Maurizio Bianchi Mattioli Nicolas Nefiodow Clara Pugsley Men Yushan
Client	City of Boulder, Boulder Public Library
Structural	Studio NYL
Civil	JVA Consulting Engineers
MEP	Design Mechanical
Lighting	Tillotson Design Associates
Graphic Design	afreeman design
Public Art Installation	Daily Tous Les Jours
General Contractor	Fransen Pittman
Photography	Bruce Damonte

The two Pilares buildings are a collaborative project with the Mexican architecture firm of Ignacio Urquiza Arquitectos, and a contribution to the Mexico City Government's series of community spaces formally called the "Puntos de Innovación, Libertad, Arte, Educación y Saberes." The Pilares seek to bring opportunity to vulnerable and underserved neighborhoods through recreational and educational programming, providing safe and active spaces for the various communities they serve. The buildings' colors—created by integrating pigment into structural concrete—are inspired by the vibrance of the surrounding buildings. Stairways connect a series of interlocking floorplates, conceived as flexible, yet dramatic, spaces lit by skylights and large, strategically placed openings. Programs include a cyber school, a robotics lab, a screen-printing studio, cooking and jewelry workshops, as well as adaptable spaces that serve everything from political activism to sports. Each building opens onto a small plot of adjacent, previously unused city land to allow for outdoor programming.

Year	2023
Location	Lomas de Becerra and Azcapotzalco, Mexico City, Mexico
Size	5,000 SF
Design Partner	Ignacio Urquiza Architects
Project Team	Michela Lostia di Santa Sofía Eder Hernández María del Mar Carballo Ana Laura Ochoa Anet Carmona Noé García León Chávez Fernando Tueme Sacha Bourgarel (IUA Ignacio Urquiza Arquitectos)
Client	Gobierno de la Ciudad de México + ZV Studio
Structural	BVG
MEP	BVG + Ecomadi
Lighting	APDA
Landscape	Genfor Landscaping
Photography	Ramiro del Carpio

PILARES
PARA EL BIENESTAR

PILARES
PARA EL BIENESTAR

The Rhode Island School of Design Student Success Center is composed of an addition and significant renovations to a historic building in the heart of the school's Providence campus. The new center provides spaces for learning, gathering, community . . . and also mail. The need to provide a central space for package delivery for students led to the transformation of a small parking lot at the rear of the existing building into a "post office for the twenty-first century." Inside, a mail recycling program allows students to break down cardboard boxes and packaging materials, to be reused for their modeling and art experiments. Outside, large windows on to the mail room and a multiuse auditorium space connect the school and campus to the city.

The project embraces flexibility, with multipurpose spaces that can transform into galleries, performance spaces, or classrooms, including including two rooms that can be combined or separated, or can disappear, using acoustic curtains. The new center also features the campus's first gender-inclusive bathroom, which was created in collaboration with QSPACE, a research group focused on LGBTQIA+ issues.

Year	2019
Location	Providence, Rhode Island
Size	21,000 SF
Project Team	Yongsu Choung Troy Lacombe with Nevin Blum Silvia DeLisi Silvia Marega Joyce Zhou
Client	Rhode Island School of Design
Structural	Odeh Engineers
MEP	Wilkinson Associates
Lighting	Tillotson Design Associates
Graphic Design	2x4
General Contractor	Shawmut Design and Construction
Curtain Manufacturer	Gerriets International
Photography	Bruce Damonte

The Miami Museum Garage transforms a parking garage façade into vertical public space by expanding upon Miami's history of architect-designed "screens" for parking structures. Designed within a permitted five-foot projection, the Museum Garage becomes a joyous opportunity for social interaction by incorporating a wide variety of environments and experiences. The new thickened envelope hosts stairways to move up and down, a gallery for graffiti art, a children's play area with a slide and climbing net, a palm tree garden, a DJ platform, benches for sitting, a lending library with built-in folding seats for reading, a listening lounge, a bar, a sloped rooftop auditorium, and a space for pets to get a drink of water—all painted Miami Vice-inspired pink. Carved into an urban "ant farm" that exposes different activities during the day, the perforated metal screen becomes transparent at night, exposing the garage slabs and cars behind.

Year	2018
Location	Miami, Florida
Size	15,000 SF
Project Team	Hyuntek Yoon Sam Dufaux with Göran Eriksson Yuchen Guo Trevor Hollyn Taub Yue Zhong
Client	DACRA and Terence Riley
Architect of Record	Tim Haahs, THA Consulting
Structural	THA Consulting
Lighting	Speirs + Major
General Contractor	KVC Constructors
Façade Contractor	Zahner
Photography	Imagen Subliminal (Miguel de Guzmán + Rocío R. Rivas)

Building B, part of the Mission Rock Master Plan developed by Tishman Speyer and the San Francisco Giants, reimagines the workplace by fostering a seamless connection between interior and exterior spaces and promoting a healthy live-work balance. Across its eight stories, verdant cascading terraces animate the building's façade. Taking advantage of required setbacks, these balconies—open to the sky—create the perfect spaces for outdoor meetings, presentations, or yoga classes, as well as relaxing oases for a midday break on even the lowest floor. As the gardens increase in elevation, the landscaping changes from leafy vegetation to hardy, wind-resistant succulents.

The LEED Gold building's extra-large energy-efficient windows allow natural light to reach the depths of the offices. Its ground floor features a visible sewage recycling and pump station that treats wastewater and repurposes it for non-potable uses across the new neighborhood and its fourteen buildings. The street level also hosts warm public alcoves recessed into the building's façade for quick meetings, long breaks, or meals from one of the local restaurants.

Year	2024
Location	San Francisco, California
Size	320,000 SF
Project Team	Matt Voss Troy Lacombe with Zahid Ajam Nevin Blum Ania Yee-Boguinskaia Leslie Dougrou Vildana Duzel Poyao Shih Christopher Stoll Hena Wang Maurizio Bianchi Mattioli
Client	Tishman Speyer and the San Francisco Giants
Architect of Record	Adamson Associates Architects
Structural	Thornton Tomasetti
MEP	ACCO, CMI, PAE
Sewage Treatment	Brightworks
Lighting	Pritchard Peck
Landscape	GLS Landscape
General Contractor	Hathaway Dinwiddie
Façade Contractor	Clark Pacific
Photography	Bruce Damonte

Marea is a sixty-unit residential development conceived at the intersection of landscape, urban design, and architecture. At the edge of Batroun, Lebanon, one of the oldest cities in the world, the new community uses density to promote a sense of collectivity, intermingling a variety of unit sizes and types that span a wide price range to increase affordability. Green roofs cascade down to the shoreline in rows, organized so that each row looks out to the Mediterranean over the roof of its neighbor. The angled forms of the tiered houses simultaneously mimic the peaks of the mountains behind and the waves of the sea below. The rows are separated by planted "streets" connecting the units and providing communal access to the public beach on one side, and private gardens on the other. The tallest row, toward the street, has the smallest units—but also the best views from rooftop terraces. The public restaurant at the beach and the footpaths that weave through the neighborhood create spaces for interaction between residents and visitors.

Year	2021
Location	Batroun, Lebanon
Size	250,000 SF
Project Team	Maurizio Bianchi Mattioli with Eyub Acikgoz Nevin Blum Nathalia Galindo Alana Rodgers Dequan Spencer Ericka Song Joyce Zhou
Client	Jamil Saab & Co.
Marine Engineer	Adessa
Architect of Record	Adel Imad
Landscape	Jack Nader, Exotica
General Contractor	Jamil Saab & Co.
Photography	Bruce Damonte

Villa Papillon was designed for a Lebanese art collector and his family. The house is composed of a series of rooms organized around an open-air courtyard. The main living space and bedroom face the sea, the family room, dining room, and kitchen open onto the courtyard. Above, the children's bedrooms look out over the living room, so that every space has a view of the Mediterranean.

At the rear, solid walls face the public walkway, while in front, glass façades featuring sliding doors open the house fully toward the water. Interior spaces are organized by a series of walls running perpendicular to the shore, allowing unobstructed sea views in every room and showcasing the extensive art collection. Each wall becomes its own object, dividing the living spaces while also containing a staircase, cabinets, or other domestic infrastructure, including the HVAC system.

Louvered steel and aluminum trellises continue the folded form of the green roof over parts of the courtyard, specifically angled to provide shade in the summer, while letting sun in during the winter months. The triangular formal language of the villa's roof planes is carried continuously across the building, patio, pools, and surrounding landscape.

Year	2021
Location	Batroun, Lebanon
Size	4,400 SF
Project Team	Maurizio Bianchi Mattioli with Eyub Acikgoz Zahid Ajam Nevin Blum Nathalia Galindo Ericka Song
Client	Tony Salamé
General Contractor	Jamil Saab & Co.
Photography	Imagen Subliminal (Miguel de Guzmán + Rocío R. Rivas)

The Adams Street Library is the first new Brooklyn Public Library branch to open since 1983. Extensive, architect-led community outreach within the neighborhoods of Vinegar Hill, the Farragut Houses, and Dumbo indicated that spaces and programming for children were lacking, and that these were important to residents across the diverse neighborhoods. As a result, the design elevates children by raising their reading room several feet above the ground, placing youth in a position of prominence. This reading room contains spaces for learning activities, story time, reading, and views out to Brooklyn Bridge Park.

Built within a historic former munitions factory, the project pays respect to Dumbo's architectural legacy, maintaining and exposing heavy timber ceilings and patinaed brick walls. Curved cutouts in the ceiling create space to hide mechanical equipment and lighting, combining new shapes with old textures. The graphic "LIBRARY" sign on the exterior is inspired by historic painted signs on warehouses in the neighborhood and designed in collaboration with graphic designers Linked by Air. The project celebrates accessibility with a vibrant universal ramp that doubles as a place for children to play and brightly colored gender-inclusive restrooms for the public.

Year	2021
Location	Brooklyn, New York
Size	7,000 SF
Project Team	Evgeniya Plotnikova Troy Lacombe with Zahid Ajam Nevin Blum Ania Yee-Boguinskaia Giorgia Cedro Leslie Dougrou Kelly Lee
Client	Brooklyn Public Library
Structural	LERA
MEP	DOSE Engineering
Lighting	Tillotson Design Associates
Graphic Design	Linked by Air
Cost	Costrak Consulting
General Contractor	Shawmut Design and Construction
Photography	Bruce Damonte

LIBRARY

The Kew Gardens Hills Library sits at a transition between bustling urban activity and quiet residential streets and serves a culturally rich and diverse neighborhood with foreign-language collections in Chinese, Hebrew, and Russian. The building is organized around a core of book stacks and service spaces wrapped by a thick perimeter of bright and open reading rooms. A green roof controls runoff and, through a series of folds, becomes a visible part of the street façade and a neighborhood feature. A 200-foot-long structural beam forms the perimeter of the building, rising to broadcast the library's activities and lowering as the building meets the smaller scale of its neighbors. At the site's main corner, the library reaches a monumental scale appropriate for its civic status, while a smaller peak marking the kids' corner provides child-size views to the south. Continuing to the back of the library, the green roof becomes a garden where tomatoes and blueberries grow.

Year	2017
Location	Kew Gardens Hills, Queens, New York
Size	10,000 SF
Project Team	Sam Dufaux Anne Menke with Jason Anderson Erica Goetz Karl Landsteiner Jesung Park Evgeniya Plotnikova
Client	Queens Public Library
Structural	LERA
MEP	Lilker Associates
Lighting	Tillotson Design Associates
Graphic Design	Epigraph Studios
General Contractor	S&N Builders, Inc.
Photography	Bruce Damonte

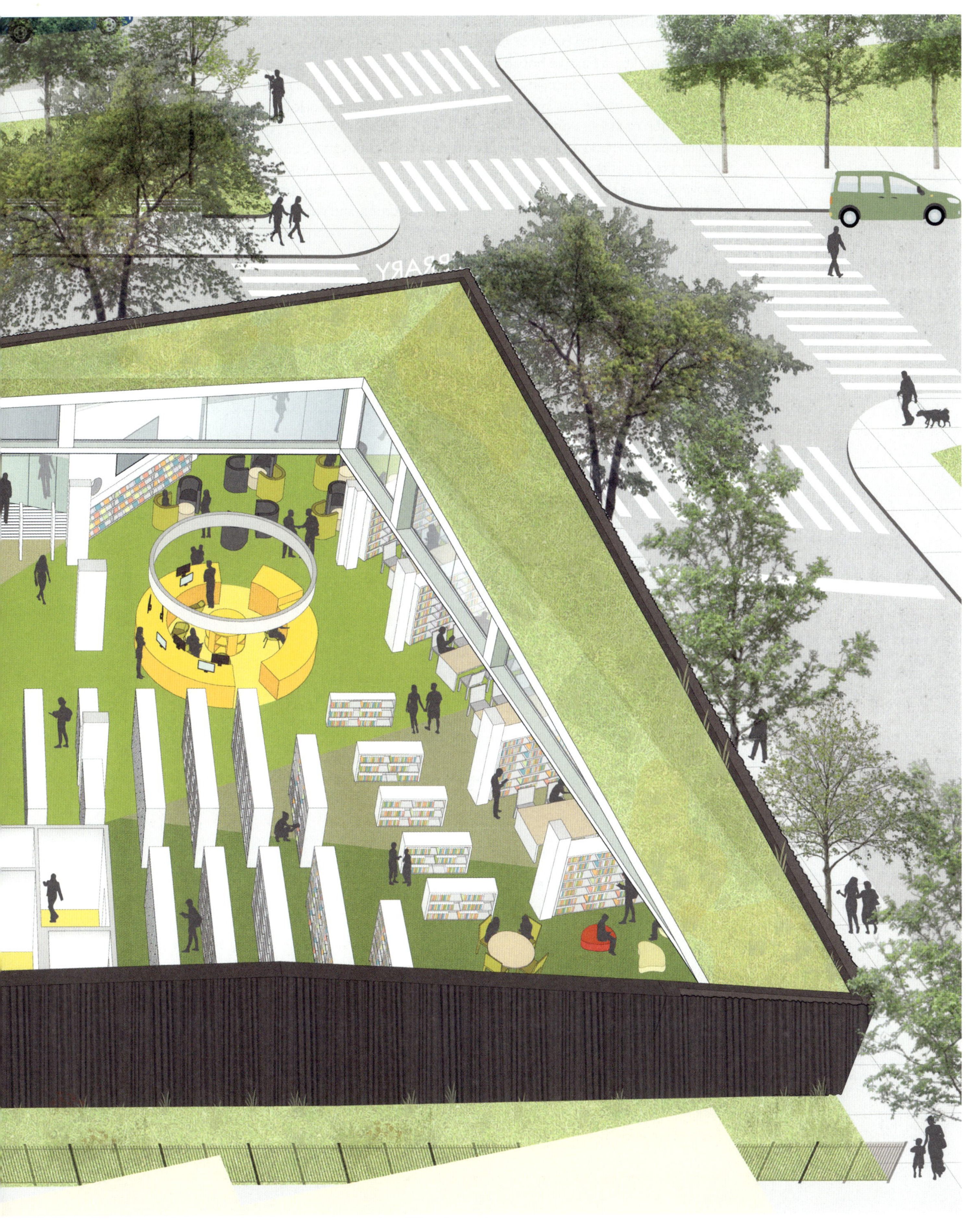

The Riverhouse is Amale Andraos and Dan Wood's house and studio, nestled in a forest on the banks of the Pawcatuck River. It is an experiment in sustainability: a passive house on a budget. While passive houses are often thought to require limited glazing and to be completely sealed, this net-zero house has been engineered to maximize window sizes and create multiple connections between inside and outside. These connections include an aperture that opens the studio to a deck overlooking the river and a roof terrace that cantilevers above the kitchen, allowing views up and through to the sky from the studio. The project utilizes sustainably grown timber, local resources, and wood-based insulation to lessen the environmental impact of both construction and habitation.

Organized around a single multipurpose "Big Room," a series of intimate-scaled rooms are arrayed around the house, each with its own views to the forest and river. Three outdoor showers are distributed throughout, celebrating year-round living in nature.

Year	2025
Location	Hopkinton, Rhode Island
Size	3,200 SF
Project Team	Kristina Dittrich Matt Voss with Reuben Cheeks Din Din Ryan Fagrie Jenna Hussain Madha Nawal Smiley Scott Rondela Spooner Henry Wotowicz Men Yushan
Client	Amale Andraos and Dan Wood
Structural	Augeri Engineering
MEP, Passive House, and Sustainability Consulting	Jordan Goldman, Zero Energy Design
Lighting	Tillotson Design Associates
Landscape	Anne Penniman Associates
General Contractor	Alan Hill and Eze Bongo R&R
Concrete	Cagin Concrete
Electricians	Bruce Kenyon and Kurt Holman
Excavation and Civil	David Benn
Metal Roofing and Cladding	Jason Senior
Plumbing	Ron Zanella
Photography	Bruce Damonte

Collaborators

Inside Outside, Petra Blaisse
Curtain

MOS, Michael Meredith and Hilary Sample
Metal table

Aronson's Floor Covering
Custom rug

Elodie Blanchard
"Ezat" tree sculpture

Suppliers

Rakks
Adjustable shelving

Sub-Zero, Wolf, and Cove
Appliances

Duravit
Bathroom fixtures and fittings

Americana Thermally Modified Hardwood
Cladding

BlattChaya, Lebanon
Concrete tiles

FSB North America
Door handles and door pulls

Sunward Steel Building
Events pavilion

Hastings
Faucets

Lutron
Lighting controls

Illuminico
Lighting supplier

OVI Ébénisterie, Montreal
Millwork

Newport Solar
Solar

Cascade Coil Drapery, Oregon
Stainless steel curtain

Fenêtres MQ, Montreal
Windows and doors

Buildings for People and Plants

. . . and Art

A conversation between Amale Andraos and Dan Wood and Heidi Zuckerman

Heidi Zuckerman is CEO and Director of the Orange County Museum of Art, a podcast host, and the author of the four-volume Conversations with Artists. Heidi has been a sounding board, a collaborator, and a client over the twenty-plus years of WORKac. In addition to participating as one of Heidi's first podcast guests, we have had an ongoing series of discussions with Heidi about the relationship between art and architecture. These conversations have influenced our thinking—not just about our art projects such as the Beirut Museum of Art, but about our approach to architecture and design—and life in general. As the BeMA project begins construction in 2025, we recently sat down with Heidi to try to get to the heart of how we view the intersections and divergences between these two disciplines.

HZ How does art inspire your practice and why do you think it matters?

AA Art does many things. Art makes you look at things differently, understand things differently. This is something that we try to do in our work as well. A feeling of discovery or surprise and not taking things for granted is definitely something that is important to us. There is pleasure in art, a sense of depth and beauty in life, which we also try to bring to our architecture. Art can give you the sense that life is deeper and more beautiful. One learns to value life through art. We try to make work that is serious, but also joyful and that has a certain generosity to it.

DX Our position as architects is, in many ways, very different from the position of the artist. We work in large teams, we work on commission, we are bound by a whole system of physical, economic, and legal constraints. Art, on the other hand, is nothing besides creativity—there's no real function and very few constraints. What we are always trying to bring to architecture is that sense of artistic freedom and creativity, the sense of an "artistic life" even within all these constraints.

AA As an artist, you're pursuing a set of questions through different works and the different times to create a body of work. We also have a set of questions that we explore from one project to the next. There is a thread, or a series of threads, that we try to make room for even within those constraints.

DX In our work, we are always trying to make projects that do more than one thing, that address larger or more conceptual issues, or that add to a sense of wonder or beauty in the world. This layering of ideas is also something that comes from the world of art. We love the idea that you can look at a piece of art and you can move on . . . or you can intensify this experience the longer you spend with it. More time with art means more to feel and to understand, and that's something we try to build into our architecture.

HZ One of the things that I talk a lot about with art is: "the more you look, the more you see." I really like this sub theme to your work, which is the idea of "the bonus" that a client gets when they work with you.

You talk about it as efficiency or an economy of means, but it's really about art. There is a value proposition to your architecture, and it's not just about maximizing the budget. It's about maximizing the brain trust, the commitment, and the experience.

One of the things that happens in art is that there's a clear moment where the artist decides "this is done." It's a little bit different with architecture because you have your initial design, your conceptual design, and then you have to price it and whatnot. But how do you relate to that idea of doneness, knowing when a project has hit that kind of perfect pitch?

AA We still make models because that's all that's left for architects in terms of artistic creation that is not digitized and that we can refer back to as the essence of a concept. For us, models serve the role of capturing that moment where things are really clicking. They are the moment of knowing when the architecture becomes art.

Photography is also important. The moment a building is photographed, it's done. That's closure for us. It's very rewarding to have a record of the project, and it also makes it easy to move on to the next one. It's also great to revisit a project long after it's complete. With our public buildings, we can go back to them many years later and see how they are being used and being lived in—and being transformed.

An artist can't control how long people are going to spend with their work, but in architecture, we can be sure that people are going to spend a lot of time in the spaces we design. As a result, we really want to make sure that we give them something to make all that time worth it. DX

For example, we always seem to put at least one circular window in our projects, and it's always amazing how much more interesting it is to people, and how much more time people spend looking out of a circular window than they would out of a square window. Our contractor for the Riverhouse used to send us progress update photos, and he would always include a picture looking out the circular window. The actual window never really changed after he installed it, but in each picture the trees would change, or the weather, or he would angle his camera a different way. For us, getting people to spend more time looking out a window is already very rewarding.

I wanted to end by talking about buildings for art. You've designed several libraries which can have art in them. You've designed community centers, which are places to make art and show art and be art. And of course you have designed galleries and the Blaffer Museum and have been working on the Beirut Museum of Art (BeMA) over many years. What kind of buildings do you think art likes to live in? If you're designing a building for art, what should it look like? What does it need? What does it feel like? HZ

For us, a building for the display of art should be a dialogue between types of spaces. Galleries themselves should not be overwhelming and need to provide a suitable, neutral backdrop for the art to be experienced. That is really important. At the same time, everything around those spaces should also be art in and of itself. We are always looking for ways to combine very simple, beautiful spaces for the experience of art with spaces around them that allow for experiencing life in a creative way. AA

With the Beirut Museum of Art, we achieve this with the exterior balconies, which form a kind of vertical and public sculpture garden that is part of the exterior envelope. The interior, on the other hand, has simple, beautifully proportioned spaces for the display of art. We are always trying to do both.

We've also designed spaces for people who live with art, including ourselves, and when you live with art you understand that it is fairly resilient. Even if you look at "real" art museums, like the Frick or the Louvre, you see that they combine spaces designed for residential uses with art spaces. The art is often piled up vertically on a wall, or sometimes displayed in a circular room like in the Uffizi, or displayed against fabric, like in the Hermitage. There is an aspect of informality in living with art that is interesting, and it can be valuable for people to understand that art is not always this specialized experience that can only happen in a specialized space. Art can also be part of life. DX

At BeMA, the sculpture garden is about experiencing art as a kind of trajectory, but it's also about showing the city that this is a place of art, and that art is part of the city, and it's part of life. We are able to have both of these ways to experience art—and artists can choose whether they want to respond to the conditions of this outdoor space and really engage with it, or simply have their works there. AA

The owner of Villa Papillon is an art collector with a very eclectic collection. He is always moving pieces around and commissioning new pieces. He is also really interested in furniture and design objects, and the architecture itself revolves around an outdoor courtyard filled with lush tropical plants. The indoor and outdoor spaces and art and furniture are all on top of each other. You see there how resilient art is. It's just a different way of thinking about what types of space are appropriate for art. There you are immersed in an environment in which art is only one part of a complex whole.

HZ I love that. And I love this idea that art and life are one and they don't have to be separate. And that is very much true in your work that architecture and life can be one, and the idea of making buildings for people, plants, and art is very much a way of really wrapping everything that you create into a comprehensible way of telling the story.

AA People seem to make the same arguments over and over again. For us, art is not a luxury, exhibition-making is not elitist, and if the artist says it's art, it's art. We have to deal with similar things. Sometimes, architects have a preconceived notion of what "serious" architecture looks like, or what a building like a museum should be like. To us, architecture can look like whatever the architect who makes it says it should look like. That will be the hill that we die on. It's about intention. If you say it's architecture, it's architecture.

Beirut Museum of Art, Beirut, Lebanon, ongoing

Amale Andraos

Amale Andraos is a cofounder and principal of WORKac as well as a Professor and Dean Emeritus of Columbia University's Graduate School of Architecture, Planning and Preservation (GSAPP), and the first woman to have become dean of the school. During her tenure as dean, Andraos also served as Architecture Advisor to the President and Special Advisor for Columbia's Climate School. Andraos is recognized as a thought leader, contributing widely to the field through her lectures and writings. Her publications include The Arab City: Architecture and Representation, coedited with Nora Akawi. Andraos has served on numerous juries, advisory boards, and selection committees. She currently serves on the Advisory Council for the New Museum's incubator space New Inc, in New York. She recently served as the chair of the Aga Khan Award for Architecture, and on the board of the Architectural League of New York. Andraos was born in Beirut, Lebanon.

Dan Wood

Dan Wood is a cofounder and principal of WORKac, a Fellow of the American Institute of Architects (AIA), and the former Vice President for Design Excellence of the New York chapter of the AIA. Wood is a licensed architect in the states of New York, Rhode Island, and Colorado and is LEED certified. Wood has taught extensively, most recently at Columbia GSAPP, and as the William B. and Charlotte Shepherd Davenport Professor at the Yale School of Architecture. He held the 2017 Frank Gehry International Visiting Chair in Architectural Design at the University of Toronto and the 2013–14 Louis I. Kahn Chair at the Yale School of Architecture. He also held both the Trott and Baumer Visiting Professorships at the Ohio State University's Knowlton School of Architecture and the Friedman Professorship at University of California, Berkeley. Wood is originally from Rhode Island.

Miles Hardingwood

Miles Justice Hardingwood is a writer and creative from Brooklyn, New York. He is a 2023 National Student Poet and a 2022 NYC Youth Poet Laureate Ambassador. His writing has received a Scholastic National Gold Medal and an American Voices Medal, and he has performed at venues such as the White House, the Schomburg Center, the Metropolitan Museum of Art, the Nuyorican Poets Cafe, and Vice President Kamala Harris's Black History Month Celebration. He attended the Kenyon Review Young Writers Workshop and the Iowa Young Writers' Studio, and he currently attends Brown University, where he is pursuing a concentration in Literary Arts.

Nicolai Ouroussoff

Nicolai Ouroussoff is currently writing a book on architecture, culture, and politics from WWI to today, to be published by Farrar, Straus and Giroux. He was the architecture critic of The New York Times, where he wrote widely on architecture and urbanism in the United States, Europe, Asia, and the Middle East, and where he was twice a finalist for the Pulitzer Prize. Previously, he was the architecture critic of the Los Angeles Times, where he was a finalist for the Pulitzer Prize for a series on the cultural decline of Baghdad. He lives in New York.

Heidi Zuckerman

Heidi Zuckerman is a globally recognized leader in contemporary art, a prolific content generator, and a fierce advocate for Why Art Matters! In addition to being the first woman to build two art museums and raising nearly $200 million for museums, she has had hundreds of courageously authentic conversations with artists and other people she finds interesting that are featured on her podcast, with over 150 episodes produced over five years, as well as in four volumes of her Conversations with Artists book series. She also recently authored Why Art Matters: The Bearable Lightness of Being, "your bedside table masterclass in how to find a way towards understanding ourselves through art." Zuckerman currently serves as CEO and Director of the Orange County Museum of Art.

This book is the result of years of discussions with many people about the best way to follow up on our "duograph" from 2018, We'll Get There When We Cross That Bridge. From early on, we knew we wanted to focus on buildings rather than the unbuilt projects, urbanism, and interiors that filled the previous book; on images rather than drawings or text; and on an edited and straightforward presentation of the work rather than 2018's "everything and the kitchen sink" approach. In many ways, we wanted to present our architectural work as an artistic endeavor.

It wasn't until we met Julie Cirelli from Park Books that everything started to fall into place. Julie encouraged us to pursue the "art book" approach we were interested in and introduced us to Sonya Dyakova and Tom Baber of Atelier Dyakova, who have created some of the most beautiful art monographs of the past ten years and who were patient, critical, and engaged partners throughout the process of designing and creating the book.

Bruce Damonte, whose photographs are used for seven of the ten projects in the book, is a critical partner and has come to define, through his images, the way in which WORKac is perceived in the world. Miguel de Guzmán of Imagen Subliminal has also been a friend of the office and produced amazing images of our work in New York, Miami, and Batroun. We met Ramiro del Carpio in Lima, Peru, and he was kind enough to travel to Mexico to shoot our Pilares projects.

We want to extend a special and heartfelt thank you to Nicolai Ouroussoff and Heidi Zuckerman, who have both been friends of ours for years and who were very generous with their time and talents in their contributions to the book.

From WORKac, we have to thank our nephew Miles Hardingwood, who spent his summer between high school and college writing and editing the main texts; Kristina Dittrich, who helped develop the initial drawing style in a series of images for our short-lived 2020 retrospective exhibition in Brugge; Imari Monroe, who developed many of the new drawings; and Claudia Aguado Batalla, who completed the set. Daniel Confroy, WORKac's Director of Communications, is an essential member of our team and worked tirelessly to assemble texts, images, collaborators and to ensure that everything came together.

Architecture is a collective and collaborative art, and the work shown here is the result of the efforts of dozens of people. Nevin Blum joined us first as a summer intern and later returned to become a very important presence at WORKac, shepherding many projects including the North Boulder Library. Yongsu Choung led the RISD project through design, and Evgeniya Plotnikova developed the Adams Street Library; Troy Lacombe saw both projects through construction. Troy also led the Mission Rock project design process. Matt Voss was a leading voice in the office from 2019–2024 and oversaw Mission Rock, the North Boulder Library, and the Riverhouse, which Kristina Dittrich originally helped design, through construction. Maurizio Bianchi Mattioli worked closely with us on Marea and Villa Papillon; and the Pilares projects were the result of an intense, challenging, and close collaboration between WORKac and Ignacio Urquiza, in Mexico City, who made those buildings a success in the face of many challenges.

Our current office is made up of a diverse, talented, and hardworking group of individuals, who constantly give us the confidence to overachieve and outperform ourselves on a weekly basis. Thank you to Daniel Confroy, Sarah Sioufi, Claudia Anselmo da Costa, Wu Li, Kaitlin Beckham, Smiley Scott, Lalin Maholarnkij, Jae-Sung Lee, Sam Bonnell-Kangas, Jenna Hussain, Yasamin Mayyas, Claudia Aguado Batalla, and Drew Pankey Wallace.

We must also thank our families, including Farid and Aida Andraos and Linda Wood. We lost Ed Wood too early in 2020, but his boundless curiosity and desire to experience the world continue to inspire us. Lastly, nothing we have done will ever eclipse our children, Ayah and Kamil, who—despite their professed disinterest in architecture—are wonderful travel and dinner companions, color selectors, occasional model-building helpers, critics, and fans. They help us see the world in better and better ways every day.

Concept
Amale Andraos and Dan Wood

Publication Assistant
Miles Hardingwood

Proofreading
Zsofia Jilling

Visual Concept and Design
Atelier Dyakova with Tom Baber

Image processing
Dexter Pre-Media, London

Printing and Binding
Printer Trento, Italy

Production
Sophie Kullmann

© 2025 WORKac and
Park Books AG, Zürich

© for the texts:
the authors

© for the images:
see image credits

Park Books AG
Niederdorfstrasse 54
8001 Zürich
Switzerland
www.park-books.com
T +41 44 262 16 62
E info@park-books.com

Product Safety
Responsible person according
to EU regulation 2023/988
(GPSR): GVA Gemeinsame
Verlagsauslieferung Göttingen
GmbH & Co. KG
P.O. Box 2021
37010 Göttingen, Germany
T +49 551 384 200 0
E info@gva-verlage.de

Park Books is supported by
the Federal Office of Culture
with a general subsidy for the
years 2021–2025.

All rights reserved. No part
of this publication may be
reproduced in any form by any
electronic or mechanical
means, including photocopying,
recording, or information
storage or retrieval, without
permission in writing from
the publisher.

This publication was made
possible in part with support
from the Graduate School
of Architecture, Planning
and Preservation, Columbia
University.

Image Credits
Bruce Damonte: 14 (left)
17–36, 57–76, 95–114, 115–134,
155–174, 175–194, 195–216;
Ramiro del Carpio: 37–56;
Elizabeth Felicella: 14 (right);
Imagen Subliminal (Miguel
de Guzmán and Rocío R. Rivas):
77–94, 135–154; WORKac:
219–246, 255.

ISBN 978-3-03860-398-6